Malden - Old and New

For Matthew and Rachel, and their generation.

Stephen H. Day

ACKNOWLEDGEMENTS

Besides acknowledging the work of the original Photographers and Publishers of the postcards, the author wishes to thank the friends and colleagues who have contributed advice, loaned or given documents, researched details, or helped with the technical aspects of desktop publishing. In particular, the following people deserve special mention, for without their generous help and encouragement this book would not have been completed:

MR and MRS A. FLEMING

RICHARD GIBSON

WINIFRED 'IVY' HARVEY (Resident, Kingston Road)

COLIN IZOD

GRAHAM JOHNSON (Postcard Dealer)

BILL & IVY MILLS (Postcard Dealers)

MRS M. POULTER (Archivist, British Red Cross)

JUNE SAMPSON

TED STAINTON

and very special thanks to TONY DURRANT of THE MARINE PRESS

The author also acknowledges the ILEA, whose training programme and facilities provided the skills necessary to achieve the finished book.

Marine Day Publishers
64 Cotterill Road, Surbiton KT6 7UN
Surrey.
Tel: 081 399 7625

Second Impression 1992.

ISBN 0 9516076 0 X Malden — Old & New: A Pictorial History (pbk)

Printed and bound for The Marine Press Ltd.
by Alderson Brothers Printers Ltd., Hersham, Surrey.

CONTENTS

INTRODUCTION

"The social history of a parish is to be gathered from ephemeral sources rather than from formal documents"

F.S.Merryweather. June1887
preface - *"Fifty Years of Kingston History"*

1887 was, of course, Queen Victoria's Golden Jubilee year and in his book written to celebrate that unique landmark, the author rightly points out that:

"The events and changes of 50 years are so numerous that it is impossible to mention them all within such narrow limits."

In his book, which he professed was only a sketch, those limits were *"the exclusion of politics and controversies"* – a commendable principle for a chronicler who was so involved locally.

Now, a century after he wrote that preface, I find myself planning the compilation of a different "sketch" (or series of sketches), and, taking him at his word, using some *ephemeral sources* that even he would possibly not have envisaged; for the "Golden" age of picture - postcards blossomed in this country during the Edwardian era, after his death. It is only because then many people collected and preserved in albums, the new and popular form of communication, that probably all the views herein are reproduced now. The photographers and publishers that proliferated at that time, catered for a commercial market, perhaps little realising that they were thereby creating socially valuable historical records too.

Frederick Merryweather lived in New Malden at a time when changes occurred with the arrival of the railway lines to New Malden in 1846, and to Kingston in 1869; and with them, the attendant needs of a growing population of a small town surrounded by farms and common land. He was an active man within the Church (churchwarden at Christ Church) and a colourful figure in local affairs. He was also the first chairman of the Maldens and Coombe U.D.C from 1894 until his death in 1900. Just as his sketch spanning 50 years could not be comprehensive by his limitations, so this series of sketches should also be viewed for different reasons.

I have been a resident of New Malden for only 4 years. I am presenting information gleaned from old trade directories, old newspapers and more worthy local historians' works, to support each postcard view – itself a frozen moment in time captured by the Edwardian photographer. And all of this brought together in retrospect by some 70 to 80 years! Therefore, if Mr Merryweather's assertion is true, this book could at best be considered ***one** of the ephemeral sources from which the social history of this parish is to be gathered.* And at worst, it is a *formal document* – an amalgam of works by various authors, designed by committee.

In compiling these glimpses of the past, I can only claim to have returned to the spots that inspired the original views, in order to re-photograph the scene today. Although in some cases due to traffic or buildings, and the wide-angle lenses apparently favoured by the early photographers, not the *exact* spot. Retracing those steps, consulting old trade directories and other records for accurate dates, and generally piecing together this "ephemeral jigsaw" gave me much enjoyment. I hope you will gain as much pleasure when looking through this book with the rather predictable title ***– "Malden – Old and New"***

Stephen Day

FOREWORD

A local history publication should be carefully researched. It should also quote its sources, be accurately but interestingly written and, ideally, provide even the most knowledgeable readers with a new perspective. Alas, few meet all - or indeed any - of these criteria.

Malden Old and New is a notable exception. Not only does it provide everything I demand from a book of this kind, but it does so in what I believe to be a unique way; for I know of no other history of this area that tells its story through rare vintage postcards. Furthermore, Stephen Day has skilfully linked past with present by photographing those same locations as they are today. Some scenes remain remarkably unchanged. In others the comparisons are odious!

I particularly admire the way he has judged the text, allowing the pictures to provide the main narrative, but adding brief captions whose concentrated detail and unpretentious style will engross everyone, be they reading for pleasure or for serious study of a locality which, like the Kingston area as a whole, has always been under-researched by local historians.

I hope Stephen Day will let us share his unique postcard collection, and his obvious love for his subject, in future publications.

June Sampson
Features Editor, 'Surrey Comet'

POPULATION *of The Maldens and Coombe from census figures printed in the book 'Village London', and from other reference material.*

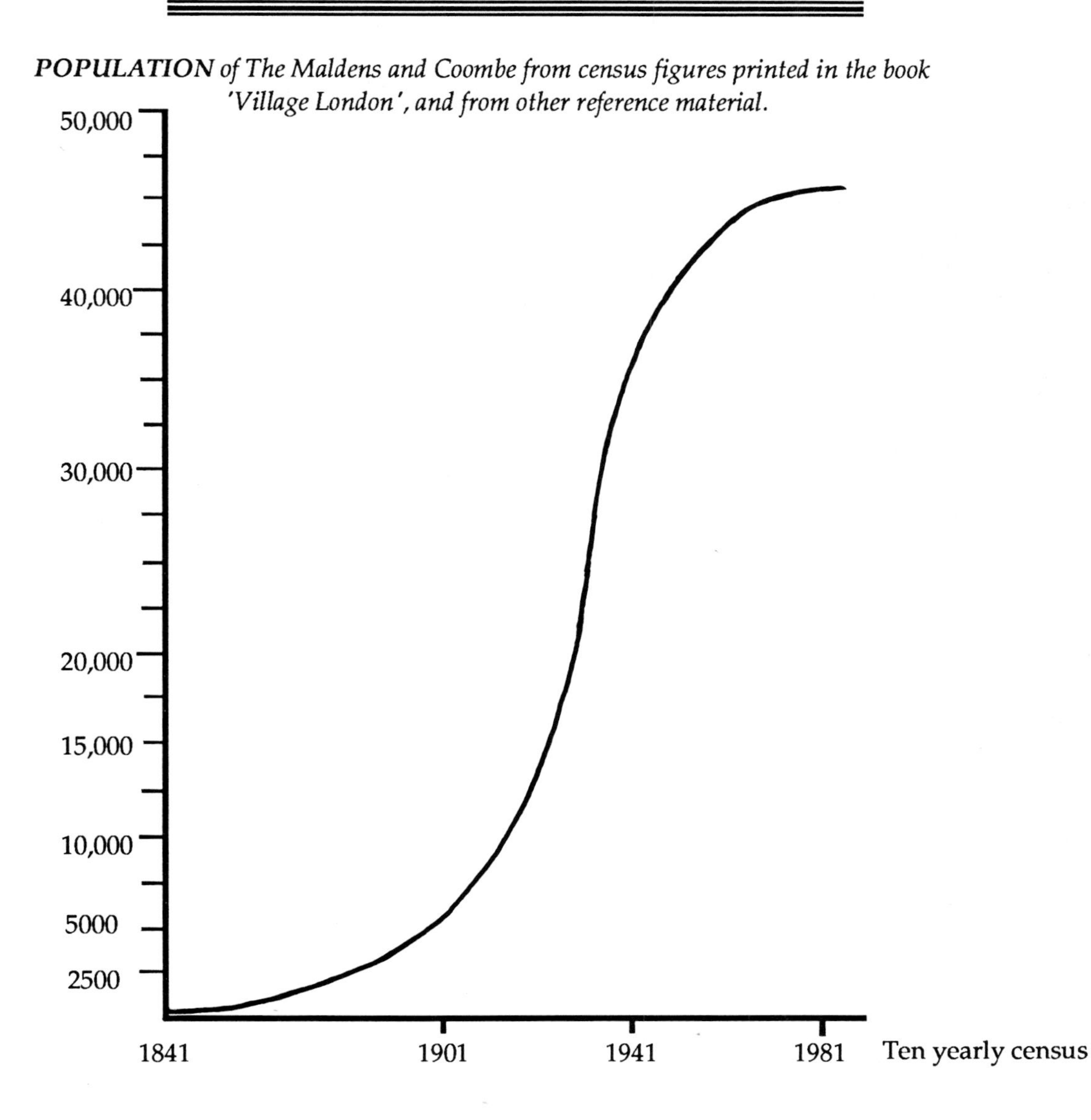

Original Publishers of the Postcards - some notes and dates.

A.S. Series - This was probably the *Artistic Stationery Company* which provided both print and photographic cards over many years from the early 1900's

BABB, - Walter Richard Babb., *Confectioner, Stationer & Library at 133 Kingston Rd. New Malden,* between pre - 1921 and 1940 (Gaps in year sequence for local directories prevented better dating accuracy)

COLLECTORS' PUBLISHING CO. - *42/44 Imperial Buildings, Ludgate Circus, London. E.C.* This was one of the largest distributors/agents for topographical postcards for S.W.London. It originally had offices in Fleet St. and the Company was active between 1901 and 1907. The "MERCURY" series was the name printed on cards issued by the firm, to distinguish their *own* publications from others they handled.

HARTMANN - ***Frederick.,*** is most remembered for introducing the 'divided back' postcard around 1902. His company published many types of cards between 1902 - 1909 from their London headquarters at *45 Farringdon St.,* including some topographicals included here. [*see also* ***T.THOMAS***]

HIDE & Co. *New Malden. Photographers &c. Address: 17 Malden Rd.* (On some earlier postcards *W.HIDE., Bookseller, 17 Market Place, New Malden.*) This was William Hide whose business, started in 1876, remained at the one address for 50 years. Kelly's directories also show that he was the verger at nearby Christ Church for 10 years from 1895.

HUTCHINSON & Co. *Wimbledon.* Brief reference to this company found in Trim's local directory for 1908/9. The address given for that year was *76a Hartfield Road.*

JOHNS - R.J.&Co., *171 Longley Rd. Tooting.* A prolific photographic card publisher who covered much of the London area between 1911 and 1935. In 1987, many of his estimated 25,000 different glass negatives were discovered in the loft of a house in Mitcham, having survived remarkably well the variations of temperature and humidity, dust and dirt, not to mention the bombs of World War 2! [*See article in "Picture Postcard Monthly', June 1988.*]

J.T.B Series - *John T. Butterfield, photographer, Cheam Rd. Worcester Park.*(Kelly's 1907/commercial section)

KINGSWAY REAL PHOTO. Series - this was a contemporary trade name for W.H.Smith's postcards.

KIRK - Art Publisher, New Malden. *Charles Joseph Kirk F.R.P.S.* Photographic Art Publisher between 1898 & 1912. Address: *The Art Photographic Works - "Clovelly" (in 1905, became numbered No.152) Mount Pleasant, Elm Rd.* [Next door at *"Summerfield"* lived Henry H.Hide - ***see page 46***] C.J.Kirk was also Chief Fire Officer [*see inset right*] from 1936 onwards for the Maldens & Coombe U.D.C. fire brigade, having started as an ordinary fireman in about 1898 when the brigade's horse-drawn appliance was kept at No.1 Acacia Grove.

MUNDAY - Henry. *Photographer.* In 1907, lived in rooms above the shops shown on page 47. He used the flat roof there as a vantage point to take many dated, (*and other local*) event cards. He never apparently identified his plates/cards, but his work must be here.

PAYNE - J. - *Stationer and Newsagent, 3 Market Place, New Malden.* (later No.6 Malden Rd.) from 1911 to 1923.

THOMAS - T. *The Library,*(sic.) *New Malden. Bookseller and Stationer at 4, Coombe Parade* (became No.19 Coombe Rd.) between 1905 and 1917. Monochrome series bearing his name was actually published by ***HARTMANN,*** [*see above*] and examples carry that trade mark.

Chief Officer of Fire Brigade.
(Captain C.J. Kirk F.R.P.S.)

OLD MALDEN

The Bridge, Old Malden Fields *(Publ: A.S. series no. 193 Colour litho print. Postally used 1905)*
There was only one bridge crossing the Hogsmill River in the vicinity of St John's Church shown on maps from 1866. A footpath crossing the fields and bridge, linked Malden with "Talworth" (as it was then known) until well beyond the 1900's when this card was used. A map of 1932-3 shows a new, shorter footpath crossing the later bridge [*shown below*] which was sited further downstream where the river meanders less. The newer footpath connected the developing housing estates of Malden and Surbiton on either side of the Hogsmill River - which today remains the natural Urban District boundary.

Old Malden Lane. *(Publ: Hide & Co. No. 22685 Sepia litho print. Postally used 1914)*

This is one of several very similar cards from various publishers of the time, featuring the Parish church through the trees. Returning to the same spot now, it is usually difficult to see the buildings for the trees. Old Malden Lane today remains a narrow thoroughfare for the traffic using it, and in most places still has pavement on one side only for anyone brave enough to venture out with a baby in a pram!

Below: The Tolworth end of Old Malden Lane will have changed far more than the Malden end, as it has had to cope with an ever-increasing volume of traffic bypassing the A3 roundabout junction at Tolworth.

Old Malden Lane, Tolworth. *(Publ: A.S. series no. 17. Real Sepia Photo. Postally used 1912)*

A peep at Old Malden Church. *(Publ: Hide & Co. Real Photo. Postally used 1910)*

This view across the field to the church is from Sheephouse Lane c.1900-10. What remains of that field and path, is today obscured by trees and dense undergrowth beside the Hogsmill Walk. The distant figure seen on the footpath had a view of the church similar to the one shown below - also difficult to recapture now, although the Manor Farm buildings to the left of the church have survived. An equivalent view today, would be possible from the homes in Percy Gardens.

Old Malden, Surrey *(Publ: Anon. B/W litho print. Postally unused. c.1900's)*

Old Malden Church *(Publ: A.S. series no. 189 B/W litho print. Postally unused. c.1900's.)*
The name Malden is derived from the *site* of this church of St John the Baptist. The Saxons were believed to have been the earliest worshippers here, and gave the site the name *"Maeldune"* which means 'The Cross on the Hill'. The Domesday Book of 1086 records the name as *Meldone*. Most of the present church building dates from the early part of the seventeenth century, with some medieval flintwork remaining in the chancel which was rebuilt, together with a new nave in 1875. Many postcards of the church at the turn of the century, show the tower and walls covered with ivy - long since removed.

Plough Inn and Pond. Old Malden. *(Publ: Hartmann/T.Thomas B/W litho print. Postally used 1905)*

The scenes on these facing pages were taken from almost the same position, but at different times of the year. The wintry scene [*right*] must have been taken after the one shown above, as the tree on the extreme left of the pond railings has disappeared. The Plough Inn was a Hodgson's (Kingston) Brewery house from 1854 until the firm was taken over nearly 100 years later, by the Courage Group. The landlord in Edwardian times was a Mr Henry Aspin, who was still in charge when the postcard on page 14 was used.

The Plough Inn. Old Malden*(Publ: JTB series; embossed 'Butterfield, Worcs. Park'. Real Photo. Postally used 1906)*

The earliest part of this old inn dates from the 15th century and it still has some of the original flagstones remaining. It is known to have been used as a 'store' for contraband on the way to London, and inevitably became associated with local highwaymen such as Jerry Abershaw and Jack Tibbett who frequented places like Wimbledon Common and Putney Heath. Since those days, various discoveries have been made about this and nearby buildings, which tend to reinforce the traditional image of the 'wanted' but elusive highwayman.

During building alterations in the 1920's on the west side of the building, a small secret shaft was discovered - the flat above the pub. has an escape 'hatch' which leads from the bedroom, goes down the back of a chimney and emerges beside a fireplace - this exit apparently, was once covered by a cupboard.

In his book *'A History of Malden'*, Kenneth Ross makes an alternative suggestion - that the necessity for a hiding place at the Plough Inn was brought about by the Civil War. And on page 93, the author has an account of the discovery of a secret room in cottages in Church Road, opposite The Plough:

'In 1944, a flying bomb landed nearby causing damage to these cottages, and workmen doing subsequent repairs discovered stairs leading into a tiny room, 7 feet square by 9 feet high. A small window in the roof had been tiled over.'

This group of cottages is believed to be of 18th century origin, and the theory is that Nos. 28 and 30 were originally one house, with the possibility of the deliberate concealment of the tiny room during its construction.

Further speculation that The Plough and the hidden room in these cottages were once linked by a tunnel beneath the road, has not been substantiated.

(Information compiled from articles in the 'Wallington Advertiser' of 24th August 1984 and the 'Surrey Comet' of 28th October 1988)

The Plough, Old Malden *(Publ: Hide & Co. No. 22688 Sepia litho print. Postally used 1913)*

Although used somewhat later in 1913, this card is probably of earlier origin, since the tree at the corner of the pond railings has re-appeared! *(see pages 12 & 13).* Through the trees on the left it is just possible to make out one or two buildings on Malden Road.

Below: Plough Green, the old village pond, and the junction of Church Road with Malden Road, today form one of several conservation areas in Old Malden. The Plough Inn is a Grade ll listed property and is now run by - appropriately - *Harvester* Restaurants.

Old Malden. -The Splash, Old Malden Lane. *(Publ: Collectors'. Colour litho print. Postally unused. c.1900)*
This view was taken looking down what is now called Church Road. The Plough is over your left shoulder, and the railings shown partly 'enclosing' Plough pond [*- see also pp.12, 13 and 14*] form a wide enough gap at the pond's edge, to allow a horse and cart to enter the "Splash", in order that the horse could have a short rest and a well-earned drink. The railings were installed around the pond in 1869 at a cost of £10-17-6d. (The job of cleaning out the pond at the same time was deferred, as the cost would have been £35-5-0d.) A 1950 local guide book has a photo. with the original railings still in place.

Below: Today, a metal fence surrounds the pond last dredged and cleaned during 1977.

Blake's Lane. Malden *(Publ: A.S. series no.188 B/W litho print. Postally unused. c.1900's)*

Located near the A3 roundabout off Malden Road, Blake's Lane is shown, if not named, on maps of the 1860's. Charles Blake, a solicitor by profession, was the local landowner then. He lived on his 130 acre estate, employing a farm bailiff and 9 labourers, between 1861-87. Often seen leading the local stag hunt, he became known as 'Squire Blake', thus giving his name to the lane leading to his farm - "Blue House" Farm. The site of the farm buildings was on land now ringed by Blake's Terrace, West Barnes Lane and Barnes End - near Motspur Park Station.

Below: It is difficult today, to be sure of the exact point from which the above view was taken.

New Malden Blakes Lane *(Publ: Collectors' /Hide & Co. Colour litho print. Postally used 1905)*

The picture below was taken at the "dog's leg" bend in Blake's Lane, looking in the direction of Motspur Park. That is not to say that it reflects *accurately* the postcard view above, since a picture taken from the reverse direction would also show a right-hand bend disappearing out of the picture. There are no buildings or landmarks on this card which usually give a reference point to help identification. Judging by the old maps of the time, the course of Blake's Lane has changed little over the years, and this is the only place in the lane where either of those directional views might have been recorded.

Beverley Schools New Malden *(Publ: Johns. Real Photo. Postally unused. c.1929/30)*

Beverley Central Public Elementary School [Boys], Blakes Lane (to give it its full, original title) was opened in 1929/30 and this postally unused card is probably of around the same date. It is interesting that the publisher has used the word 'Shools' in the caption - not just for the obvious spelling mistake, but for the use of the plural - as if there was more than one department? The railings seen around the playground area formed the boundary to the surrounding unused land. With the inevitable encroachment of outbuildings over the years, that boundary gradually widened to border the Kingston bypass, and the picture [*below*] had to be taken from the nearby footbridge over the A3, to be able to convey today's nearest comparative view.

"Coombefield" New Malden, Surrey *(Publ: Anon. Real Photo. Postally used 1954.)*

This was one of several large, late Victorian houses situated in Malden Road. *Coombefield* was opposite the junction with Blake's Lane. The same site, near the main A3 roundabout, is now occupied by the flats in Wickham Close. [*shown below*] The old house survived the construction of the Kingston bypass, opened in 1927, as it is still shown on maps of the early 1930's. However, local street directories show that from 1934 the name *Coombefield* was no longer given as the address, - the house had become numbered '207' Malden Road.There is no further mention of the house after the entry for 1938, so it appears that the house was demolished after that. However, this postcard of it was not 'postally used' until 1954!

From an old photograph c.1920/30

This photograph shows a cart-track which was known as *Sow Lane* on the map of 1866. The view has changed more, probably, than any other in this book. Pictured standing on his plot of land to the left, is a bearded figure, indicating the site where his house is to be built. The faint line of trees in the distance would later become the approximate course of the Kingston bypass.

Below: The same view today. Houses in South Lane, near its southern junction with the A3 Malden Way.

NEW MALDEN

Malden. - The College *(Publ: Collectors' "Mercury" series. Colour litho print. Postally unused. c.1900's)*
This distinguished building set in its own spacious grounds, was sited alongside Malden Road opposite the junction with Thetford Road. Mr Alfred Streeter, a resident of New Malden, became 'proprietor' of the college in 1884. Until 1914 it was a boarding and day school, and then had a spell as a wartime clothing factory. Ten years after the Great War ended, between 1928 and 1932, it was called *St. George's College,* but reverted to its original name when it re-opened in one of the big houses on land now occupied by St. James' Close. The A3 trunk road eventually brought about the end of Malden College on this site.
Below:Welbeck Close now occupies the original site, but these two views should not be compared *directionally.*

Thetford Road New Malden *(Publ: Anon. Real Photo. Postally unused. c.1900's)*

This view, taken looking towards Malden Road, shows the location of Malden College quite clearly. Its characteristic belltower can just be seen in the distance, between the tall trees of the college grounds. The gateway entrance to it off Malden Road, is right opposite the junction with Thetford Road.

Norbiton Park Hotel, New Malden, Surrey. *(Publ: Anon. - probably KIRK. B/W litho print. Postally used 1905)* On the left is the original fountain, erected in 1894, and after which the Norbiton Park Hotel [right] was re-named in 1929-30. In the distance is what is now the High Street. The building behind the flag is the police station - the land for which became New Malden's most expensive site at £500, when purchased in the late 1880's. For over a decade earlier, serious wrongdoers had had to be accompanied on foot to Wimbledon, Kingston or Epsom police station. This led to allegations that hooliganism and some minor offences were being overlooked by the Constabulary! Opened in 1892, the new station afforded no excuses.

Malden Fountain *(Publ: Babb. Sepia litho print. Postally unused. c.1915-20)*
This must be one of the Publisher's earliest cards and it can be dated to sometime *after* May 1914, when a loose timber from a passing horse-drawn load damaged the original fountain, causing the gas lamp on top to be replaced by a double one. (The fountain was completely removed in 1932, following accidental demolition by a motor van). The horses drinking from the trough, have drawn the Bentall's removal cart along the length of Kingston Road - which appears to be missing its tramlines. {*Probably re-touched photograph*}
Below: Today, a traffic island stands almost on the site of the old fountain. (A refuge for pedestrians in place of the refuge for animals?)

Tram Terminus New Malden *(Publ: Anon. Real Photo. Postally unused. Date: 1906)*

The postcards on these two pages were published by the same unidentified author, if the handwritten captions are anything to go by. And judging by the interest shown in the tram by the onlookers above, the year would be 1906 when the service commenced between Hampton Court and the Fountain, New Malden. Trams were routed via Norbiton Church, Cambridge Road and Kingston Road - and the fare cost 2d. Comparison of this scene with the very similar, but later view on page 29, shows the addition of a pillar box and signpost at the near corner of the 'island' terminus.

Tram Terminus New Malden *(Publ: Anon. Real Photo. Postally unused. Date:1907)*
The interest shown here by onlookers, is probably because of the newly extended tram service to Raynes Park. The tram's destination indicator on the front, top deck would appear to confirm this. Only one year previously, the trams had had to terminate here.
Below: The Fountain roundabout has seen many changes in Public Service Vehicles using it over the years. Following the trams in the 1930's came trolley buses, which were themselves finally replaced by petrol and Diesel-engined buses during the 1960's. Today, one of the main routes - the 131 - is a privatised service, operating a fleet of mainly green vehicles.

First Tram New Malden. *(Publ: Anon. Real Photo. Postally unused. Date:1907)*

Although trams from Kingston commenced service in 1906, they terminated at the Fountain. On 27th April 1907, the first extended service to Raynes Park started, as the destination board on the tram arriving at the junction of Kingston Road and Malden Road (now High Street) indicates. This card records that *later* event. The large house on the corner is now the site of Ketts electrical store, and the tramlines lead into Burlington Road. The long arm of the law is raised as the tram approaches the crowd assembled to witness a milestone in public transport history.
Below: Almost unrecognisable, today's equivalent view from the police station at the Fountain roundabout.

New Malden *(Publ: Johns No.6310 Real Photo. c.1920's)*

This card shows almost exactly the *reverse* view of the camera angle used on the page opposite. The large house on the left obscures the view of the police station at the corner of Burlington Road. The site of the original fountain directly in front of the Norbiton Park Hotel, can be seen clearly.

Below: A new fountain was installed on the roundabout in 1982 after a gap of fifty years. It cost £23,000.

Flower Show New Malden July 19th 1911. *(Publ: Anon. Real Photo. Postally used 1911)*
Both of these cards have been included because they show local people, but their actual *locations* are a mystery. The author of the card above, records that he/she *'obtained one 1st and a 3rd place out of 5 entries at the show yesterday, not so bad considering the awful weather - not for roses.'* Postcards of the event were apparently ready the next day!
Below: Street directories show that Thomas Watt, Builder, lived at No.2 Sussex Rd. New Malden, from 1908 when this card was sent to *Harry Hoad* in Vancouver, Canada. The sender (Jim)...*'thought you might like to see a few of the old faces'* which perhaps meant Mr Watt [*centre?*] and his workmen, were *Harry's* ex-workmates seen at a new site? Although Sussex Road houses date from 1908, the frontage of these homes is a little different.

Kingston Road, Malden.

KINGSTON ROAD

Kingston Road, New Malden. *(Publ: Anon. Real Photo. Postally unused. c.1906-10)*

Kingston Road pre-1910 looking east, at its junction with on the left, Elm Grove (now Elm Road) and right, Westbury Road. When the shops in *Albany Parade* were erected in 1910, at the corner with Elm Grove [*see below and page 34*] the tram stop seen above, was re-sited away from the adjacent corner. The Baptist Church on the right dates from 1891.

Kingston Road, New Malden. *(Publ: Anon. No.113 Real Photo. Postally used 1916)*

A similar view, taken just a little further west along Kingston Road than on the page opposite. The site of *Albany Parade* shops is hidden by hedges and trees, which have also almost obscured the re-sited tram-stop plate on the nearest conductor pole (seen just above the gent's straw boater hat!).

Below: Today's bus stop and shelter appears to be on exactly the same spot as it was some 70 years ago.

Kingston Road New Malden *(Publ: Hide & Co. Real Photo. Postally used 1910)*

Trade Directories for 1910 list these shops as *Albany Parade* - so named after the next road along from their *actual* location - at the corner with Elm Road. On this card , only six of the eventual block of eight shops have been built, four of which are occupied and 'in business'. They are from left to right: **No.1 J.E.Williams; Grocer/General Store** *(137- 'Cycle Shop)*. **No.2 W.G.Thompson; Family Butchers** *(135-Butchers)*. **No.3 C.H.Manton; Greengrocer** *(133-Electrical)*. **No.4 W.Hornby; Dairy** *(131-Grocery)*. By 1911, **Carl Elster; Baker,** had opened at **No.6** *(127-Baker's)*.

(Information in brackets shows today's numbers and businesses.)

Malden Baptist Church, Kingston Road. *(Publ: Babb. Colour litho print. Postally unused. c.1920's)*

Malden Baptist Church, erected in 1891 to replace the previous smaller, and simpler chapel that had been on that site from 1875. In August 1940, German bombs destroyed this building and the present church [*shown below*] was built there in 1953.

The publisher of this card, Walter Richard Babb, had his confectionery/stationery shop opposite the church at No.133 Kingston Road (now an electrical business). This address followed the re-numbering of the *Albany Parade* shops in 1911, into the Kingston Road sequence.

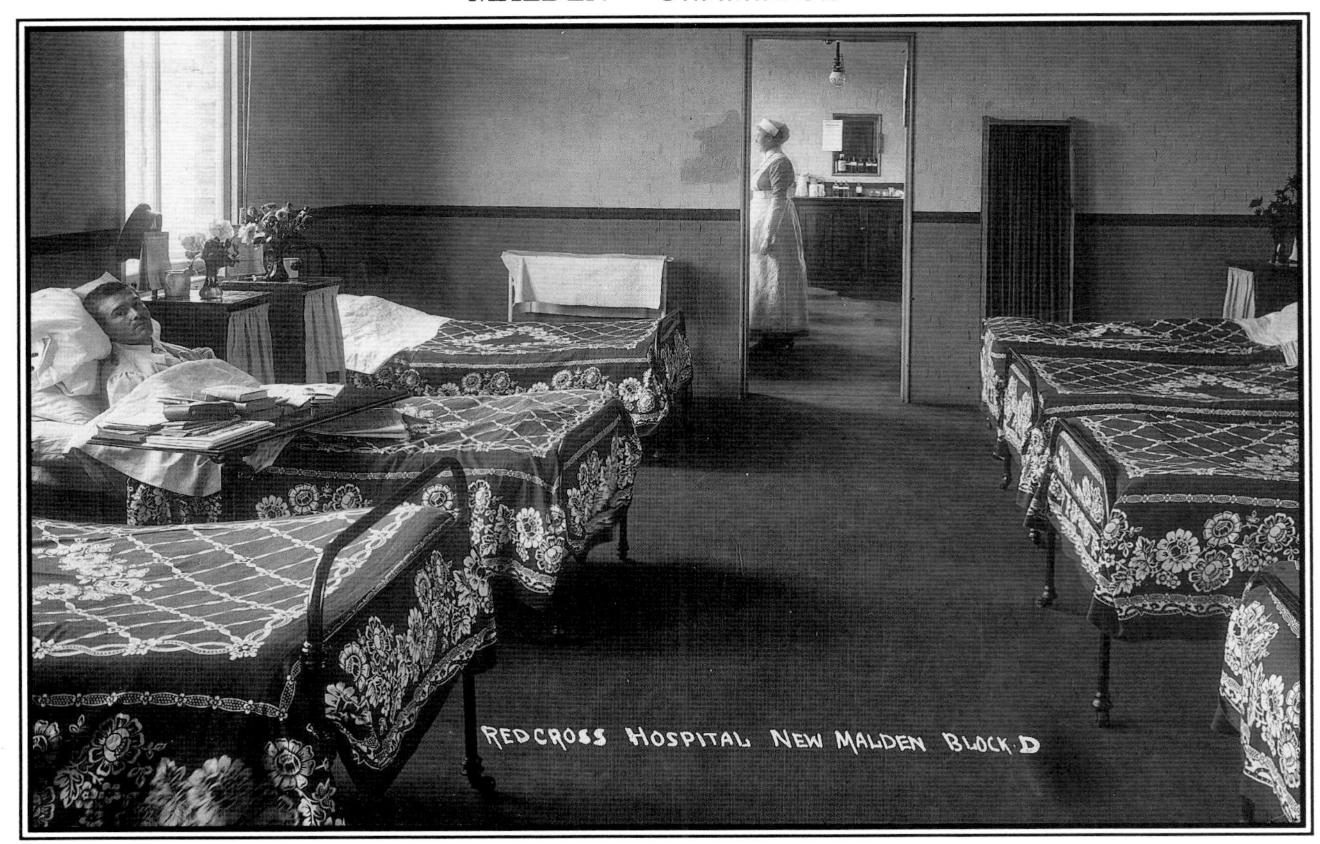

Red Cross Hospital New Malden. Block D *(Publ: Anon. Real Photo. Postally used 1916)*

The interior shot of this hospital ward wasn't easily located. However, it is recorded that the Springfield (branch) hospital in Kingston Road, was used for hospitalised Canadian troops during World War 1, with the patients in residence being moved back to Springfield for the duration. The elaborately patterned bedspreads brighten up an otherwise drab setting for the returning hospitalised heroes.

The *Surrey Comet* for August 7th 1915, has this account on page 7 :-

KINGSTON & SURBITON RED CROSS HOSPITAL.

Renovation and redecoration of the building nearing completion.
Matron appointed.

"For several weeks past, bands of voluntary workers, members of the local Voluntary Aid Detachments of Kingston, Surbiton, Ditton and Coombe have been busily engaged in the preparation of this hospital, situate at the Norbiton Common Farm, Kingston Road, New Malden. The work has been done under the direction of committees, the principal of which is the House Committee, which has the benefit of the services of Mr Henry Compton as Chairman, while this and all other committees are being served with complete efficiency by the energetic Hon. Sec. Mr A.G.Gumpert. The work that has been done includes the re-making of mattresses, the re-painting of bedsteads, the preparation of hospital linen and the furnishing of the staff apartments; and preparatory to all this, the re-decoration of the whole of the wards

---

The account goes on to say that one wing would soon be opened for use, in spite of some structural alterations delaying the full opening. Also, Miss K.E.Jones had been appointed Matron - and her comprehensive C.V. and qualifications for the job are given in detail. Medical service was to be provided by some 20-30 local practitioners sharing voluntary duties. Then follows a letter to the editor, appealing for furniture - also a piano, gramophone, records, billiard table etc. Offers to subscribe newspapers and magazines for the patients were invited too.

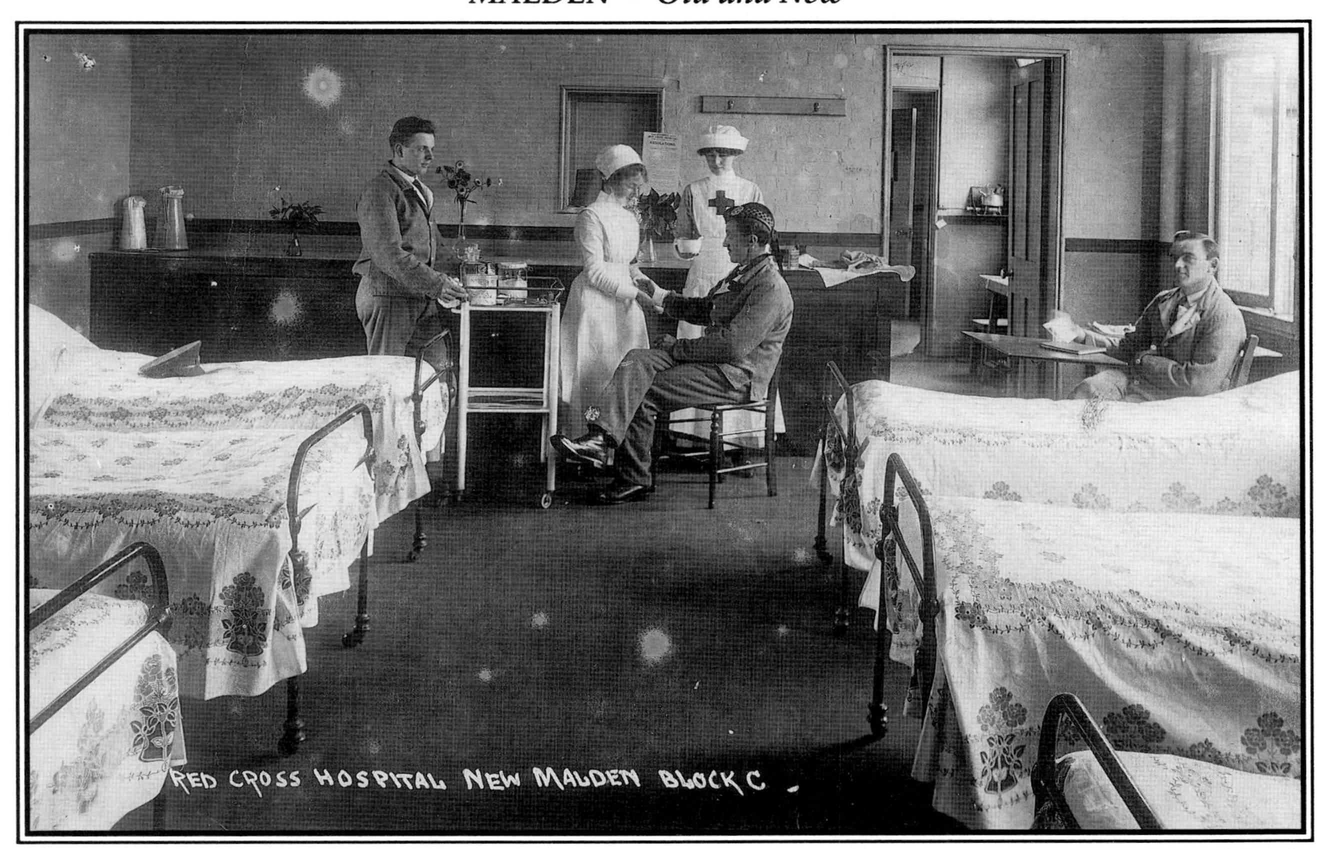

Red Cross Hospital New Malden Block C *(Publ: Anon. Real Photo. Postally used 1917)*

This postcard, published by the same anonymous author as on the opposite page, would have been taken as another in the series showing the interiors of each of the hospital block wards. From the messages on the reverse sides, the senders of both cards shown were obviously recovering here.

Below: The Springfield (branch) Hospital Kingston Road, now known as the Morris Markowe Unit, showing the blocks where the war wounded were accommodated.

A.V.F. New Malden 1914 *(Publ: Anon. Real Photo. Postally unused)*

Of all the farmland around New Malden at the time of World War 1, there is no way to be sure in which field exactly, these men are assembled as an Army (Auxiliary?) Volunteer Force. The pictures are included in this section of the book because of the wartime link with the Red Cross Hospital at Norbiton Common shown on the previous pages.

The group of officers [*below*] has been photographed against the backdrop of some houses which could give a clue to that location.

Group of Officers. New Malden A.V.F. April 25th 1915 *(Publ: Anon. Real Photo. Postally unused)*

THE 'VILLAGE'

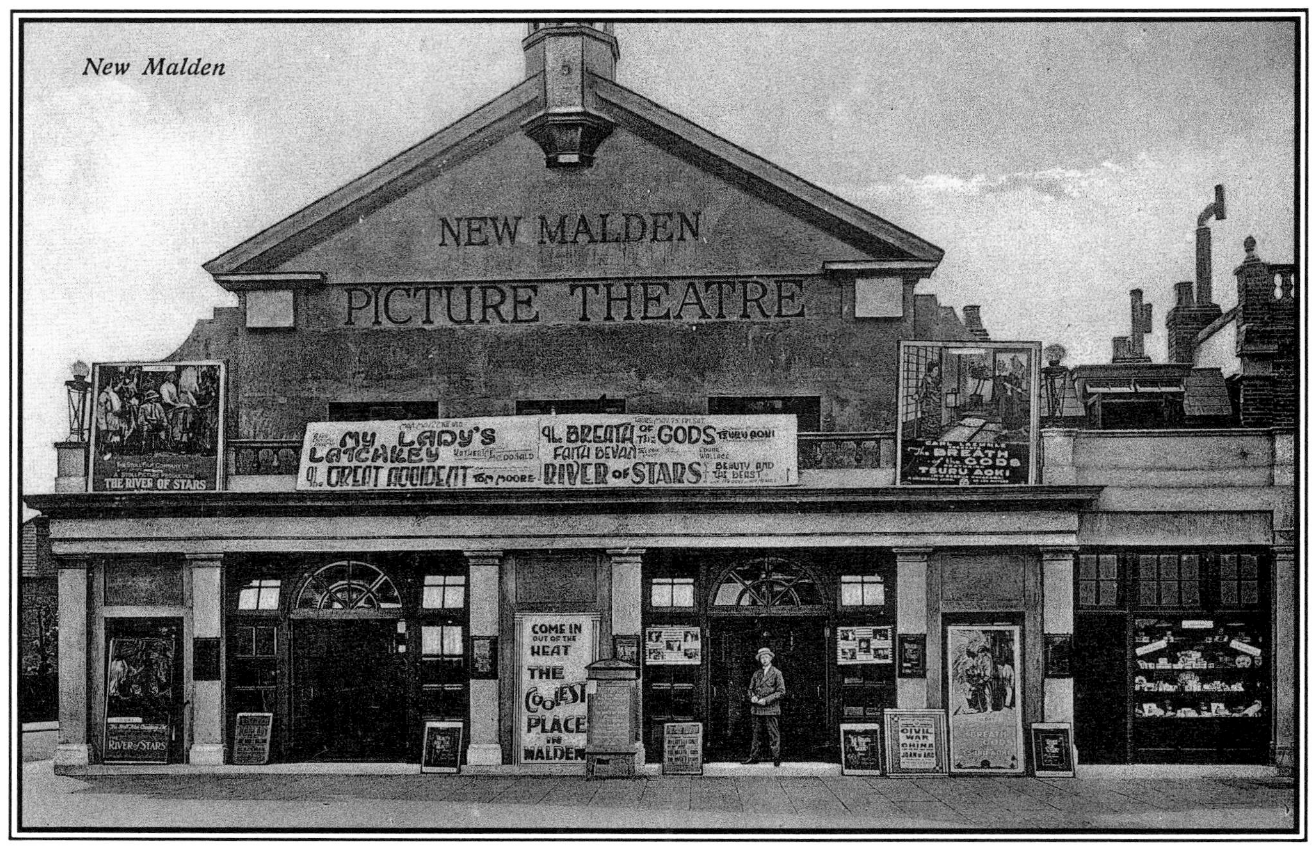

New Malden Picture Theatre *(Publ: Anon. Sepia litho print. Perf. left edge. Postally unused. Dated 1922)*

Built in 1921 at the corner of Sussex Road and Malden Road (now the High Street), this view was taken during the week of 25th May 1922, possibly during a heatwave. [The notice between the main doors invites would-be filmgoers to *"Come in out of the heat - The coolest place in Malden"*]. Seven years later, the cinema was to re-open as The 'PLAZA' [*see page opposite*]. The last films shown there were during Christmas week 1936, for in the early hours of Sunday December 27th the PLAZA burned down, never to be re-built.

Below: How many youngsters today would guess that a cinema once stood in place of their hamburger bar?

PLAZA

PHONE ——— NEW MALDEN. ——— 0263

LATE NEW MALDEN PICTURE THEATRE.

RE-OPENING MONDAY, FEBRUARY 11th, at 8 p.m.

DOORS AT 7.15.

MONDAY, TUESDAY AND WEDNESDAY NEXT.

ON THE SCREEN

REX INGRAM'S

The GARDEN of ALLAH

with

ALICE TERRY and IVAN PETROVITCH.

ON THE STAGE

HALFORD & MILLS

RYTHMIC DUETTISTS.

MUSIC

PLAZA SYMPHONY ORCHESTRA

Under the direction of MANNY SCHALET.

PRICES OF ADMISSION

MATINEE TILL 4 p.m.		EVENING AFTER 4 p.m.	
Front Stalls	5d.	Front Stalls	6d.
Front Centre Stalls	5d.	Front Centre Stalls	9d.
Centre Stalls	9d.	Centre Stalls	1/3
Back Stalls	1/3	Back Stalls	1/10
(Children 5d. & 9d.)		(Children 5d., 9d. & 1/3.)	

CHILDREN FULL PRICE SATURDAY EVENING & BANK HOLIDAY.

CONTINOUS .. .. .. 2.30—10.30
DOORS OPEN .. .. .. 2 p.m.

CAFE OPEN DAILY 10.30 a.m.—10 p.m.

From the *Surrey Comet* of 9th February 1929:

'The New Malden Picture Theatre, Malden Road, having been acquired by the Plaza Ltd., extensive alterations have been carried out internally and externally, and on Monday the Theatre is to be re-opened under the title of "The Plaza". For the special performance at 7.45pm, to which the Chairman and members of the Maldens and Coombe U.D.C., together with members of the councils of surrounding districts, and also a number of influential residents, have been invited by the management, -exceptionally interesting films are to be shown. Included amongst the improvements are admirable lighting and stage effects'.

Below: A dramatic photo. of the fire which destroyed the 'Plaza' on 27th December 1936. [Source: The Kingston Heritage Centre library]

Malden Road, New Malden. *(Publ: A.S. No. 241. Real Sepia Photo. Postally unused. c. 1912)*

This is a later version of the colour-printed card shown on the front cover, whose caption refers to this part of *Market Place* as 'The Pavement'. The shops in the parade are [*left to right*] **No.67** - W. Field & Son: Boot makers. **No.65** - The MaldenPress (Miller's) and A. Beaumont & Son, Watchmakers. **No.63** - Malden Sanitary Laundry and Greenwood, Hone & Co. Electrical Engineers. **No.61** - Ben Whitley, Draper. **No.59** - E.H.Dodd, complete outfitter. **No.53** - H. Tytherleigh, Fruiterer. **No.51** - William T. Saunders, Provision dealer. Further along, on the corner of Cambridge Road, **No.43** - Nicholas Pearce - Draper, the shop later bought by Mr and Mrs Tudor Williams.

Fire Brigade Display New Malden Nov. 1st 1913. *(Publ: Anon. Real Photo. Postally unused. Dated 1913)*

The crowd outside the Wesleyan Chapel at the corner of Cambridge Road is watching the Fire Brigade's display taking place opposite. The fire station was sited next to the Town Hall building. The year is 1913. Behind the trees, is the small, corner draper's shop (No. 43 Malden Rd) taken over earlier that year by Mr Tudor Williams and his wife Nora, which then expanded over many years to become New Malden's only Department Store.

Below: Still a family business, the Store celebrated its 75th anniversary in 1988. The present Methodist Church dates from 1932, and was built on the site of its old Wesleyan predecessor which had been erected in 1867.

Market Place New Malden *(Publ: A.S. No. 186 B/W litho print. Postally used 1904)*

Today's only remaining buildings from this card view of 1904, are the row of shops (with blinds) up to Grafton Road, and the signal box now dwarfed by Apex Tower. In 1904, the shops from the extreme left to right were: **1**)Thomas Montague:*Baker/Grocer.* **2**)W.G.Sudbury: *Ironmongers.* **3**)F.J.Hawkins: *Fancy Repository/Post Office.* **4**)J.C.Giblett:*Butcher.* **5**)H.H.Hide:*Drapers[see p.46]* **6**)Wood & Hill: *Wine & Spirit Merchant.* On the opposite corner of Grafton Road was S.E.Fisher:*Oilman [see p.47]*. Of the shops listed, it is interesting to note that two of them retain the same retail trade today. They are: *Craftsmen-Ironmongers*(Sudbury's) and *Victoria Wine Co.*(Wood & Hill)

New Malden - The Market Place *(Publ: Collectors' B/W litho print. Postally unused: c.1900's)*
Market Place in what is now the High Street, comprised the shops between the railway bridge, to the corner of Cambridge Road and beyond. The card on p.42 shows that next parade referred to as 'The Pavement'. In this 1900's scene of the *other* side of the road, it extended to Duke's Avenue. All that remains today though, is the bank, and what was the small shop alongside.[*see p.49*] What had been Holy Trinity church on the far right, was finally demolished in 1989 to make way for the new Waitrose Supermarket premises, which was also designed to incorporate the facade of the old Town Hall as its main entrance. The nameplate *Market Place* is still in situ today, above the Victoria Wine Co. shop shown on p.46.

Draper's Shopfront. *(Publ. Anon. Real Photo. Postally used 1908)*

Written in 1908 by (Mrs?) J. Daw, this card was produced to advertise the shop, which had changed hands in1907 after 31 years, when Edric G. Daw bought the 'Linen Drapers' business from Henry Hawkins Hide, a resident of Mount Pleasant. Directories show that Edric Daw traded here until 1940, but by this time the address had 'changed' from simply *Market Place,* to become 25 Malden Road. Note the three large gaslights over the windows and door. The original real photographic card is so detailed that individual price labels on the goods in the window can be read with the aid of a magnifying glass.

Below: The same site exists today, but as the Prudential Estate Agency near Grafton Road.

Fisher Shopfront *(Publ: Anon. Real Photo.- badly faded, No.201 Postally used 1908)*
On the adjacent corner of Grafton Road (once called *Providence Place*), stood **Fisher's - Family Oilman** (signified by the large jars on the roof) - an ironmonger's store. In 1900, Mr S.E. Fisher took this shop over from **Grant's** until 1917, and is seen here in the doorway, many of his wares displayed outside - everything from a tin bath and ladders on the left, to stone hotwater bottles and shopping bags on the right. Outside gaslights are prominent again. Next door, the window of the **Devonshire Dairy** shows that they supplied 'Rich New Milk' from nearby Hoppingwood Farm.[*see pages 54-55*]
Below: Shops at the base of the office block '*Apex Tower*' which was erected on this site during the early 1960's.

Market Place New Malden *(Publ: Anon. No.4073. Real Photo. Postally unused. c. 1908 - 10)*
In the High Street near the station, the area once known as *Market Place* has seen most changes, especially since the early 1960's, when the town's skyline changed dramatically with the addition of a tower office block on either side of the road. In this animated scene of circa 1910, most people have stopped to gaze at the camera. The shopfronts between the station and Duke's Avenue then comprised from right to left: *Charlie How*, Outfitter: *International Tea Co's Store Ltd*: *William Waslin*, Hairdresser/tobacconist: *S.R. Easter*, Motor & Cycle Works**[wheel sited on wall above shop]**:*William Francis*, Corn & Coal Merchant**[shopblind]**: *Clement Bowry*, Cowkeeper & Dairyman: *A. Aggiss*, Butcher: *Fredk. Cheeseman*, Coffee Room: *Daniel A. Sweeney*, Wine and Spirit Merchant.
Below: St George's Square fronts the *C.I. Tower* block, today's view necessarily being taken from across the road.

London and South Western Bank *(Publ: Collectors' "Mercury" series/Hide & Co. Colour litho. Postally used 1908)*
Apart from the obvious change of name of the bank to 'Barclays', there is apparently little change to this view at first glance. Adjoining the bank used to be a chemist's shop - that of Francis C. Mathews MPS - and this was acquired as the bank expanded its premises. The old shop frontage now houses the bank's automatic cash dispenser. Next to this was the Holy Trinity Church, built in 1883 of stone to replace the original 1870 iron structure. Ten years later however, this building closed *as a church* and was eventually bought by Mr Graham Spicer initially for use as a boy's Bible class and Institute. Since then, it has always been known as the Graham Spicer Institute, and only recently was it replaced as part of the new Waitrose supermarket development.

Below: Behind the bank, today's new Graham Spicer Institute has been erected nearby, in Duke's Avenue.

Coombe and Malden Railway Station *(Publ: Anon. Real Photo. Postally unused. c.1910)*

The creation of New Malden, and its subsequent development was due entirely to the arrival of the railway. The station, originally called *'Malden for Coombe'*, later became *'Coombe and Malden'* - and it was not until the late 1930's that the name *Coombe* was dropped altogether. Opened in 1846, it came in for much criticism in the early days - the buildings and surroundings giving a poor first impression of the town, repulsing potential newcomers and some visitors. When she arrived to visit the gentry of Coombe, Queen Victoria preferred to alight at Norbiton! The views here were taken from the footbridge linking Alric and Duke's Avenues. The central platforms appear to be the busiest [*above*], and these days, are only used to give staff access to the original signal box.

COOMBE ROAD

New Malden, - The Market Place (II.) *(Publ: Collectors' "Mercury" series. Colour litho print. Postally used 1907)* This view along Coombe Road looks towards Traps Lane from the station. Across the road is the Railway Hotel. A Thorne's Brewery House in Edwardian days, it was rebuilt before 1890, but dates back to an early homestead of the 1850's. The area designated *Market Place* obviously extended both sides of the railway bridge, to cover the shops etc. shown above. In fact, a guide book of 1950 for Malden and Coombe tells us that when *The Groves* developed as the first roads near the new station, this area just north of the railway line was '.....for some time, the centre of the town'. The Kingswood Chemist 's shop, from near where the photo below was taken, originally housed *The Cinematograph Theatre* (later called New Malden Cinema Hall) - the town's first, small cinema.

Coombe Road, New Malden *(Publ: Anon. Real Photo. Postally unused. c.1940's)*

This is the reverse view of the card opposite, but on a much later postcard. Although unused postally, the back of the card had incendiary bomb damage information pencilled in to match the letters A. B. and C marked on the shop and station buildings shown above, thus dating it to around the time of the second World War. The shops on the left had originally been known as *Coombe Parade* when built between 1900 and 1910. Wilshere's confectionery shop on the corner of Alric Avenue must have been there for years, as it is recorded in a street directory for 1912. In all the early postcards which show the railway bridge, it is interesting to see how narrow the arch was until widened to its present size during 1959-61.

Hoppingwood Farm, New Malden *(Publ: A.S. No.182 B/W litho print. Postally used 1905)*

The original *Hoppingwood Farm* dated back to the early 1700's. Its 255 acres were split in two with the arrival of the railway line around 1835. Between 1850 and the early 1900's, the Horlick Family (of the famous hot drink) farmed here. Much of that land is now occupied by Beverley Park and Malden Golf Course.

Malden - Hoppingwood Farm *(Publ: Hutchinson & Co. Wimbledon. Colour litho print. Postally used 1907)*

Hoppingwood Avenue *(Publ: Anon. Real Photo. Postally used in 1935)*

When Alric, Cambridge, Hoppingwood, Rosebery and Orchard Avenues were laid out for housing around the time of the first World War, these new roads surrounded the site of the old farmhouse and buildings shown on the page opposite.

Coombe Wood Farm, **renamed** *Hoppingwood Farm* and shown on maps of the early 1930's, was located by the junction of Coombe Lane and the A3 Kingston bypass. It still retains some later 19th century farm buildings, including an octagonal, timber dovecote with weathervane.

Coombe Road. New Malden. *(Publ: Kingsway series No. 11820. Real Sepia Photo. Postally used 1916)*

Taken looking towards the station from the junctions with Cambridge Avenue [*left*] and Lime Grove [*right*] this photographic card has really captured something of the atmosphere of the time when life was conducted at a more leisurely pace than it is today. Not just the horses and carts, but the figure seated on the roadside bench, and the delivery man leaning on his bicycle. The photograph below was deliberately taken when there was little traffic about, so that the impact of the change of buildings is seen clearly. Whereas the postcard shows all residential buildings, today's picture is of office and business accommodation.

Coombe Road Malden. *(Publ: Anon. Real Photo. ML3. Postally used 1909)*
A similar view to that on the opposite page, but taken some 50 yards further back from just outside the Christ Church building [*left*]. Again, the onlookers and carefree cyclists indicate the sedate, village mood.

Below: Just two houses (now a doctors' practice on the corner with Lime Grove), have survived among the business and commercial premises which have gradually developed between Acacia Grove and The Royal Oak Hotel, along this side of Coombe Road over recent years.

Christ Church New Malden *(Publ: Anon. No 4038 Real Photo. Postally used 1913)*

The above view of the church, which was erected in 1866 on a site given by the Duke of Cambridge, was taken from a point near the vicarage. In recent years, accommodation improvements to this side of the building have altered the aspect considerably. The interior view below, is from a colour postcard of 1906. Note the gas lighting above the pillars (electricity didn't come to the town until 1911). Specially embossed with the words -***A Happy Christmas*** , this was a way of personalising a postcard for the recipient, on those special occasions.

New Malden Christ Church *(Publ: Collectors' "Mercury" Series. Colour litho print. Postally used 1906)*

The Vicarage New Malden *(Publ: Anon. Real Photograph. Postally used 1908)*

The author of this card makes reference to the couple in the picture. They are almost certainly the then vicar of Christ Church - the Reverend William Allen Challacombe M.A. and his wife, incumbent since 1893.

Below: The Reverend Canon John Short and his wife Sheila, kindly recreated the scene above, with their dog called 'Pepper'.

Coombe Road, New Malden. *(Publ: A.S. No.183 B/W. litho print. Postally used 1907)*

The Royal Oak Hotel shown in these two cards of Coombe Road, dates from before 1876. In both views, the tall trees behind the hotel, although recorded in different seasons of the year, have a very similar shape and number of boughs. Interestingly, *both cards* were postally used in 1907. However, the view below shows considerable alterations to the hotel's facade (which have remained to this day). It should be reasonable to assume therefore, that the improvements were made at around this time. These days, the hotel's flagpole is fixed to the building.

New Malden:- Coombe Road *(Publ: Hutchinson & Co. Real Sepia Photo. No.1032. Postally used 1907)*

Coombe Road New Malden *(Publ: A.S. No 4611 Real Photo. Postally used 1920)*

In the view above of circa 1920, the trees mentioned on the opposite page have been cut down, perhaps because they were getting too big? In today's photo, [*below*] some different trees have grown up in the intervening years.

Coombe Rd New Malden *(Publ: Johns No. 6316. Real Photo. Postally used 1924)*

A final glimpse back towards the town from the Royal Oak Hotel highlights again the changes made along Coombe Road from as recently as the 1960's, when the distant *Apex Tower* was built just the other side of the railway line. Other things don't change however: The Royal Oak still serves *Benskins* Ales; and the 'custom' of marking postcards with a cross [*as above*] to indicate to our nearest and dearest where we are staying, dies hard. In this case, the road marked is *Sycamore Grove*, which leads appropriately, into the next section!

THE GROVES

New Malden - Acacia Grove *(Publ: Hutchinson. Real Sepia Photo No.1036. Postally unused. c.1908)*
In 1850, the National Freehold Land Society bought 57 acres of land just north of the railway station, and *The Groves* were the first roads of the new town to be laid out and planted with trees to match their names — Acacia, Chestnut, Lime, Sycamore, Poplar and Elm. However, the first occupants of the houses had to contend with very primitive conditions — no lighting, no mains water and no drainage. By 1866, the medical officer reported that the whole of New Malden's sewage was carried along Coombe Road in an open ditch, the smell from which was 'almost intolerable'. Things seem more hygienic in the above view of circa 1908, — a milk-churn/handcart is in use, and gas lighting has been installed. These roads were only really wide enough for horses and carts to pass.

Acacia Grove, New Malden. *(Publ: A.S. No. 249 Real Sepia Photo. Postally used 1914)*
This view, about halfway along Acacia Grove shows 2 of only 3 bungalows in a road of quite mixed housing. At about the time this postcard was used, the comedy actor Fred Emney who then lived at No.66 Acacia Grove, was making his debut on the London stage at the age of 15. [Most people would probably remember Fred as the portly character actor of British films of the '40's and '50's. - playing a monocled, cigar- smoking, imperturbable English gent.] After his father died in 1917, he sold the house (originally known as Burlington Villa) which was eventually demolished in 1961/2 to make way for the service road to the flats in Maple Court. Fred died in 1980 of injuries sustained during a pantomime, after slipping on the soapsuds during a knockabout comedy scene.

New Malden: - Chestnut Grove *(Publ: Hutchinson & Co. No.1035 Real Sepia Photo. Postally used 1908)*
Of all the roads comprising *The Groves,* Chestnut Grove seems to have been the most popular as far as old postcards are concerned. At least six different views still turn up today. This particular one is taken from the Coombe Road end, looking towards the Poplar Grove junction. A solitary horse and cart contrasts with the line of parked cars in today's scene, which was taken in late autumn to try to show more of the houses on the left.

Below: Although most of the garden fences and gates have now gone, some large, stone pillars remain from the low-walled gardens - noticeably, next to the lamp-post [*right*], and above the roof of the third car along [*left*].

Chestnut Grove, New Malden *(Publ: Kingsway Real Photo. No. S 3018. Postally used 1909)*
This is the reverse view of that shown on the opposite page - taken *from* the junction with Poplar Grove. The tall Horse-chestnut trees must have made this end of the narrow road quite dark, even in summer. There are now only two or three of these trees surviving, near the Coombe Road junction. The only evidence of the big house and garden on the left that still remains today, is one of the high brick columns of the garden wall - and that is missing its complete globe-shaped decoration on the top. In the photograph below, this remaining pillar is just hidden from view by the street light at the centre of the picture. All the modern views of *The Groves* were taken prior to the width restrictions and ramps being introduced to control the speed of traffic in this area.

Poplar Grove New Malden *(Publ: Anon. Real Photo. Postally used 1908)*
This view along Poplar Grove was taken from the end near the railway line. The author of the postcard has marked his house with a cross for the recipient. At the corner with Acacia Grove is No. 23 Poplar Grove. This must be one of the original and best-preserved of detached houses from Victorian times. A wall-plaque near the front door acknowledges its significance. By the time the area of *The Groves* had become established around the mid-1860s, two small places of worship were located along *Poplar Walk* as it was then known. Prior to the building of the first Baptist Chapel on Kingston Road in 1875, a temporary building stood on land between the railway line and Acacia Grove on the same side as Fairmead Close. [*In the view above - it lay back, off to the left-hand side*]

Poplar Grove New Malden *(Publ: A.S. No. 248 Real Sepia Photo. Postally used 1911)*

Taken at the junction with Chestnut Grove, this postcard continues the same directional view along Poplar Grove as the previous page. Before Christ Church was built on Coombe Road, the temporary church of St James was erected in 1856-7. This was located on the opposite side from the site of the Baptist Chapel, but much further along, between the junctions with Lime Grove and Sycamore Grove [*It would have been on the right in the distance, in the above view*]. How long these buildings lasted after their respective churches were built, isn't clear. A local map of 1898 still shows *Poplar Walk*, and the location of the Baptist Chapel.

New Malden - Lime Grove. *(Publ: Collectors' "Mercury" series. Colour litho print. Postally unused. c.1900's)*
While cars may come, and horses and carts may go, some things change very little. Christ Church School [*right*] was completed in 1870, and is still in use today. The picture above, shows that part of the school building [*to the left of the tiny entrance porch*] which has now gone. In today's view below, the porch is to the left of the near street lamp, with the remaining brick building to its right. The seven Lime trees fronting the school building must have been kept well pruned back, as they have developed only a few sturdy boughs over some eighty years or so. In the foreground of the left hand pavement, a brick gate-pillar is the other obvious remaining reference point.

New Malden, Sycamore Grove. *(Publ: Collectors' "Mercury" series. Colour litho print. Postally unused. c.1900's)* This view, about halfway down Sycamore Grove, looks towards the junction with Poplar Grove when there were still ample trees to make a 'grove'. This is the only card which seems to turn up today for this road, although others must have existed. Cards of Elm Grove (now Elm Road) are also very difficult to find now. In 1857, a gasworks was established in Elm Grove. But it was not until 1868 that *The Groves* and other streets of the town came to be lighted by gas.

Below: These days, few of the Sycamores are left standing and several small blocks of flats have now replaced some of the larger houses.

Mount Road, New Malden *(Publ: Anon. Real Photo. Postally unused. c. 1915-20)*

As with Beech Grove (which connects it with Elm Road), Mount Road is not shown on original plans of 1850 for The National Freehold Land Society's layout of *The Groves.* These roads and houses were built much later - from around 1904 onwards. Each house was given a name e.g. *Ashleigh, Beechwood* etc., until numbering took place in 1911. It is perhaps surprising though, that Mount Road was not named *Birch Grove,* judging by the Silver Birch trees originally planted on either side. All of these have now been replaced, mainly by ornamental Cherry trees.

COOMBE

A corner of Coombe Warren. Coombe. *(Publ: Hartmann/T.Thomas. B/W litho print. Postally used 1904)*

The Coombe Warrens' Saga

During the 1860's many elegant houses and mansions were built in the Coombe area. Many were named after the locality e.g. *Coombe Croft, Coombe Leigh* etc. As a result, two entirely separate houses built then, were both called *Coombe Warren*. The postcards at the top of these pages show part of the Coombe Warren mansion once owned by Bertram Currie, an international banker and financier, who was also a close friend of the then Liberal Prime Minister William Gladstone. At his invitation, Mr Gladstone became a frequent visitor to the house and grounds during his four terms of office, and meetings of the Cabinet had to be held there in 1884 while he overcame illness. This particular *Coombe Warren* was demolished in 1926 leaving only a lodge and some boundary walls bordering Coombe Lane West and Coombe Hill Road.[*p.76*]

The second *Coombe Warren* was one of three fine houses which John Galsworthy had built near Warren Road. John Galsworthy junior, born in 1867 spent his infancy there. It must have been a happy time for him, for in later life, as the author of "The Forsyte Saga", he modelled one of the principal settings in the story on the site and grounds. In a letter written in 1929, he wrote: *'The site of the Forsyte house was the site of my father's Coombe Warren. The grounds and the coppice etc. were actual. But the house itself I built with my imagination.'* From 1874, almost until the Galsworthys left Coombe in 1887, the young author lived at *Coombe Leigh* the nearby, second-built family house.

Between 1875 and 1931, when it too was demolished, *Coombe Warren* was bought and sold several times. The grounds were landscaped and the house almost doubled in size to accommodate the Society parties for which Coombe was becoming world-famous. At one stage a concert hall and ballroom were added and the house aptly re-named *Coombe Court*. The list of party guests over these years frequently included Royalty - Edward Vll and Queen Alexandra, the future George Vl, the Queen of Spain, George V and Queen Mary. Prominent artistes of the period such as Nijinsky and Karsavina, Pavlova, Melba and Caruso were introduced to Kings and Queens there.Today, the site of *Coombe Warren* is occupied by two houses - *Stone Garth* and *Coombe Crest* but, like its counterpart, the old entrance, a lodge and a boundary wall survive.

Malden, - Coombe Warren. *(Publ: Collectors' "Mercury" series. Colour litho print. Postally used 1910)*
This card shows in closer detail, the same building as on the opposite page, but from further to the left so that the arch is hidden from view. Considering that almost all of this particular *Coombe Warren* mansion was demolished in 1926, it is remarkable that the postcard publishers had previously chosen, around the turn of the century, to record this small 'corner' of the large estate. Today, it along with some boundary walls and a lodge [*shown overleaf*], are all that remain of the original buildings.
Below: The archway, and gabled building with the tall chimneys [*top of pages 74 & 75*] still exist as 'Warren Close', along Coombe Hill Road.

Norbiton - Coombe Hill.

(Publ: Collectors'. Colour litho print. Postally unused. Date. c.1905)

The title of this card may be confusing. The picture is of Coombe Lane from the top of Coombe Hill where the road forks, looking towards Kingston. If the lad with the bike on the page opposite, looked over his left shoulder - this is the view he would have. This is the part of Coombe Lane West at the top of Traps Lane, where the lodge and boundary walls of the first - mentioned *Coombe Warren* estate [*pages 75/76*] can still be seen. The lodge itself is seen on the right, just before the signpost pointing up Coombe Hill Road.

Comparison of the postcard view above, with today's view from the same spot [*right*] shows little apparent change in 90 odd years. However, the photograph was taken on a quiet Sunday afternoon, and not during a weekday rush-hour, when traffic to and from Kingston and the nearby A3 can cause quite a different picture!

Top of Barings Hill, Coombe *(Publ: T.Thomas No 131761 Colour litho print. Postally used 1909)*

The top of Coombe Hill, before the road divides to form a small triangle of land with Trap's Lane used to be called Baring's Hill, probably after the prominent Coombe resident - Edward Charles Baring. Following his marriage in 1861, he and his wife found *Coombe Cottage* the perfect country retreat to escape from the stress of life in London. Despite its name, it was always a large house with over 60 rooms! A family of six children was raised there, and in 1887 their younger daughter Margaret, was married to the Hon. Charles Spencer who eventually became the 6th Earl Spencer and, through their son, great-grandfather of our Princess of Wales.

Top of Barings Hill. Coombe *(Publ: Hartmann/T.Thomas B/W litho print. Postally used 1905)*

In 1881/2, at the invitation of Edward Baring, the widowed and exiled Empress Eugenie lived at *Coombe Cottage*, following the death of her only son. There, she was often visited by Queen Victoria and other Royal guests. Four years later, following a dispute over a threatened new railway line to pass nearby his cherished country home, Edward Baring, (by then Lord Revelstoke) sold the whole estate to the railway company for a considerable sum, and built himself a comparable retreat in Devon on the proceeds. The London & S.W. Railway built a bridge and laid some track (which are still visible just off the A3) then abandoned the project.